Living Our Dreams
Book 1

Living Our Dreams

Poetry by Cheryl Spangler

Graphics/Cover by: Carrie Litten

FORBZ HOUSE, LLC
2014

Copyright © 2014 by FORBZ HOUSE Publishing

All rights reserved. This book or any portion thereof may not be reproduced or used in any manner whatsoever without the express written permission of the publisher except for the use of brief quotations in a book review or scholarly journal.

First Printing: 2014

ISBN 978-0-692-27875-8

FORBZ HOUSE LLC
7371 Atlas Walk Way Suite 142
Gainesville, VA 20155

www.Forbzhouse.com

Order Information:

Special discounts are available on quantity purchases by corporations, associations, educators, and others. For details, contact the publisher at the above listed address.

U.S. trade bookstores and wholesalers: Please contact FORBZ HOUSE, LLC. 703-348-3011 or email: forbzhouse@gmail.com

Dedication

To my mom, dad, son and daughter

Contents

Acknowledgements ix
Preface 1
"Broken Focus" 3
"13" 4
"Soul" 5
"Dreams" 6
"Love" 7
"Birds" 8
"Second Time" 9
"5 min to go" 10
"Daughter" 11
"Home" 12
"Just me" 13
"Who Am I" 15
"Energy Flow" 16
"Universal Consciousness" 17
"Song" 18
"Angels" 19
"He's the One" 20
"Shy Soul" 21
"Overwhelm" 22
"Holes in the Leaves" 23
"Openness" 24
"Chimes" 26

"Train to Nowhere" 27
"My Love" 28
"Trees" 29
"My Man" 30
"Sending Love" 32
"No Man is an Island" 33
"Independence" 34
"Selfless Hero" 35
Note from the Author: Meaning of the Coconut 37
CONTEST 2015 39

Acknowledgements

I would like to acknowledge all the people, places, animals and nature I come in contact with every day of my life, they inspire me in ways I cannot put into words.

Preface

(an opinion with no discrimination of other's beliefs)

If I want to be closer to God, I take a look at every situation and object I look at with total bliss and splendor. As I move through the day/week/month/years I hear things, see things and feel things and it inspires me to put into words my thoughts on that topic or event. This collection of poems comes from a standpoint of intense gratitude for things I experience. On my spiritual journey to remember who I am and what my soul's path is for me, I share these poems with you...a little opening into my soul.

"Broken Focus"

It's "OK" to stop! for a minute . . . she said
as she handed me her papers with a cut on her head.

are you done? Have you finished? Can you come sit with me?
I really want to show you that I only got one "B"

the focus it takes is undying, unending,
it's deep in my soul, I relent to it or it's crying.

I stop myself forcefully, breathe in and stare
I want her to know above all that I care!

all the times before now that I've told her to wait
bring tears to my eyes…After all, she's "11" now not "8"

I sit on the floor, right then and there
her in my lap, bun in her hair.

I read every word of her grades as she smiles,
listening to my excitement stopping time for a while.

and I love and I cherish these moments we have,
where success and hard work, time lines and plans,
must do and must haves, go deaf to the world
when a child has spoken.

"Thank God", I say "My Focus is BROKEN".

"13"

He laughs so hard, we tear up and cry.
my soon to be 13 year old looks me right in the eyes.

"I want to be like you when I grow up" he says "Mom"...
"you know, happy successful and strong"

I look at him and we both start to smile
he has no idea it will take me all evening to digest his words for a while.

and I realize my son who mostly stays quiet,
with his face in his screen and his thoughts to himself.

observes, listens, watches every moment in time,
to analyze his environment and his own mental health and mine.

what we learn from our kids is that nothing gets past them.
but by teaching them "Happy" we create joy everlasting.

I vow every day I will start and end with a smile.
spreading joy through the house, through my life, like a child!

"Soul"

I hear you breathe, in such a rhythm
music playing, flowing like ribbon.

wearing a hat like you do all the time.
looking beautiful every day, your hand in mine.

you see your life, you see your death.
you feel the time between and rest.

you love the people in your life.
you make amends to end the strife.

you ask yourself what could you do.
to shine a light and make it through

everything you've ever thought
has appeared before you as if bought!

you manifested every hour, good or bad,
and acted as if everything you wanted you already had.

remembering becomes easier every life you live,
when you start by asking "what is it, I have to give!"

"Dreams"

They take us home, they bring us messages,
we think we are sleeping or walking through passages.

but we are in a dream right now!
the one we asked for, the one we wished for!

to live a life where everything we wanted,
is vibrant and magical and loving ... not haunted!

living the life of our dreams means first... accepting
that each moment is a blessing not a curse.

it is then that we give from a mind that is "LOVE"
and we know we are connected to our source from above.

so lose yourself in the grass one day, think of work but go out and play,
make a friend on the corner street, check the mirror one day you'll meet.

and don't forget in a blink of an eye, your life becomes dreams starring you and I.

"Love"

It drives the brain, makes us insane,
this little word, it's just a Verb!

it's not something to be achieved,
lost or stolen, crushed or bereaved.

it's not meant to control our lives,
but instead to give us a twinkle in our eyes.

it's a four letter word we love to say
without thinking, we use it every day.

it doesn't require rings and cheer,
just believe it already exists and it will appear.

it's in our soul, can't be obtained
the window panes sometimes get stained.

one day we realize we can't see through,
the dirt in our lives keeps blocking truth

that little word that means so much,
the feeling we have from gods first touch!

"L" is for Listen, something God does with us,
"O" is for Obstacles we can crush without a fuss.
"V" is for Voices, inside our head we should listen to more often
"E" is for Eternal, a state of gratefulness that makes us soften.

"Birds"

They fly so free, they used to be
a piece of God's green earth you see.

they watch over those who need them most
and deliver messages to God as they coast.

when will we graduate to life up above?
where we can soar through the skies spreading joy and love.

a bird is a gift sent from mother earth
as she watches the human race give birth!

their feathers are soft like the clouds we can't feel,
to warm them and cushion their landing in fields.

their beaks are stretched long so to grab and to point, lead and direct,
keeping their babies and flocks completely in check.

people see birds as a sub-human species,
flying south for the winter, leaving air bombs of feces.

but they are the brains and the gifts can't be counted,
as to how many times a bird flies over head,
and another prayer's answered as you lay in your bed.

"Second Time"

Live everyday as if it were your second chance,
a redo of sorts to clear won't, don'ts and Cant's.

if you got up each morning with gratefulness in your heart,
enjoying each moment using feelings not smarts.

decisions would come to you easy and strong
like peddling a bike and knowing right from wrong

the second time around is a mindset to have
just pretend you have lived that day once before now,
so your mind can relax and not throw in the towel.

pretend this day has come and is here for you again,
to laugh some more, love someone, enjoying it to the end.

why is there a need for a glass half full or a glass half empty at all?
simply take the picture sitting beside and fill it 10 feet tall

if all the people you met today, you could greet them one more time
you would widen your smile, sit down for a while, and believe that
what's yours is mine!

and if there ever comes a day when a second time is not there,
and you have to live your life all day long once with care.

throw care out the window, make it loud, fast and fun
take a moment to dream big and smile at everyone.

"5 min to go"

It's such a rush, the time flew by,
we must get out the door before you cry.

although it seems when we first wake, time stands still
oh but then its 6:48. threw on our clothes, made bed, brushed teeth
uh! oh! We forgot something on our feet.

if only it was saturday morning we moan, when the sun comes up, we
lay in our bed and a dog gets to dream of a bone.

but our homework's not finished, I still haven't ate,
my coffee is brewing and crud its 6:48.

we know when to leave, it's the same every day
and yet instead of packing our stuff we sit down and play.

we rush to the car grabbing doggie and all
"don't spill my coffee", "wait mom, my pants are too small"

"I forgot my shoes", "I can't find my phone"
"fine!! Just leave, I'll just sit here all alone."

but we take a deep breathe collect all our stuff,
head down the road as I yell to two arguing "that's enough!"

no matter what happens inside our house in the morning,
that 30 minute drive to school is anything but boring.

we laugh at our jokes, crazy vines, new ideas!
rush in for gas grab a drink, sing to "Fancy"

our rush out the door is always welcomed I know…
because it gives me extra LOVE time to share with the kids …and grow!
so whenever you find yourself rushing to go,
remember the journey coming up and take it slow!

"Daughter"

The day you were born, I knew it was true,
birds flew overhead an angel appeared and no one was blue

everything about you was peaceful and smiles
from your pink soft lips, your bright blue eyes to your fancy styles.

It took only a moment for your brother to learn,
that his new little sister was funny and stern.

no matter where we went you were go-with-the flow,
laughing and lovin and putting on a show.

every morning when the sun comes up,
I am wide eyed to see you like a new little pup!

you are clever and witty beyond anyone I have met,
for only being "11" and 80lbs soaking wet.

the people who know you, teachers, friends, fam and dogs
get a tiny little glimpse at your heart and Monologues.

but I see you fully, with all your smarts, smiles and love,
and the wonderful peace you bring from God up above.

you are here for a reason in my life everyday,
to bring heaven to earth in a new special way.

If there's ever a time you feel angry or sad,
just remember I Love You more than life and so does your Dad!

"Home"

We think our home is this physical place,
where couches sit, dinners are served and shoes are laced.

where our cars pull in to a neat clean garage,
and we arrange our photos on the wall in a collage.

we come home every day and thank God we have a place to rest,
decorating and planting and cooking our best.

but home is a place inside each of our hearts,
where we love one another until death do us part.

It doesn't matter where, whether big or small, brick or wood, rich or poor, a home is created instantly inside ourselves …not a store.

so as you decide what to buy, where to live, when to move,
and you're scared that things will change.. schools and kids, dogs and moods!

going smaller, going bigger, in the country, in the city,
there is something you are taking no matter where you go.
that is the essence of home, embodied in you from head to toe.

where all the love and family begins to start a new life,
embrace the change, a new laid plan, an excitement that feels right.

"Just me"

I sit and I listen to other women speak,
assessing their hair, their car and their week!

should I buy a suburban, an SUV or what?
Its time for our family to make some cuts!

very complacent and happy with life,
never really thinking about much except being a good wife.

chatting away in t-shirt and shorts,
hair all a mess, no makeup and out of sorts.

a little bit of slang, a country twang, these ladies talk,
about their carpool schedule and how their kids better walk the walk.

my mind races fast thinking of all the things I want to invent,
the businesses I will start, the lack I will circumvent.

I am bubbling with abundance always ready to take on the world,
never sitting still, after all I am just a young girl.

I have plans to live to 120, life is not that short at all,
the last thing I want to do in this life is be a flower on a wall.

my ambition runs high, determined to explore,
self motivated and free, once I learn it, things seem a bore.

I am a sponge for information, soaking it up like a summer day,
and just around every corner my spirit finds it's way.

I feel a light inside me shining brighter than I can see,
an overwhelming knowing that my path has yet to be shown to me!

I feel the enormity of the universe, and how we are all connected as
one, and when we let go of our ego, the world shines
abundance on us like the sun.

"It's just me" the little girl said, standing all alone,
looking down, one hundred angels holding her above Gods throne.

you don't' have to use your eyes to see what gifts you have been given,
just open up your heart, become aware and enjoy livin!

"Who Am I"

My label is my name I have grown to love about myself,
my body serves me well because I keep it in great health.

who's eyes see what I see, they are only an extension of me,
who's ears hear what I hear, Oh...but they only work when someone is near!

I am not a sum of my thoughts, since they are created from brain and observed by self - like it or not.

I am not the objects I view, but instead the observer inside of you. I am not the feelings I feel, for they are what's created when the mind makes a deal.

get friends, be nice, dress well, fit body,
the pressures of the mind could use a hot toddy.

we set expectations the mind can't fulfill, and wonder why the chatter's overwhelming...not still.

we must get behind the objects in our mind
to be seated with the in-dwelling, the self, every time.

"who am I?" says the girl, "if I am not all these things?"
you are awareness itself...an awareness of being.

"Energy Flow"

Relax, release and keep your heart open.
experience the moment that is passing through you,
fix the broken.

stored and scarred, an energy bubble, a samscara is born.
choose to inspire, laugh and giggle so your heart is not torn.

like a leaf dropped in water, ripples begin,
flowing and rolling out and in.

so is an event that comes into our life,
out of our control, rippling past like a knife.

every event is like energy in our mind,
it has to flow in, be compiled, get intertwined.

but the energy must come out, get released, be let go,
so that we can find clarity in the moment, the self must know.

unlimited energy is available to us now,
when we sit in "the way" and allow, just allow.

there is something so peaceful when the mind stops it's chatter,
life becomes love, God is close, Nothing else matters.

when an event, or a person, a word or a thing,
clings to your psyche wrapping around like a ring.

slip it off just as easy, let the energy go,
let it burn off the stillness you maintain…and you will grow.

"Universal Consciousness"

When you are aware that you are aware, you are turning into "self",
your viewing the in-dwelling being that has been put upon a shelf.

the one that sees through the eyes you have,
the beautiful world, judging good and bad.

the one that hears through the ears you were given,
the sounds of children, birds and harmful livin.

the one that feels the emotions that drive you,
loving and frustration, happiness and sad too

the self is the one that has always been there,
like God and the sun just you have not always been aware.

like a movie, so engrossed we forget we are in the seats,
so is life to our "self", brilliantly playing with it, like wind to a leaf.

but if that leaf were to realize that the wind will come and go,
and the stem that holds it strong to the tree is embedded far below.

then the leaf would just enjoy all the swaying back and forth,
and each breeze is just events in life, that never change it's course.

the self may seem elusive, because the pull of life, the movie, is so loud, but it's sitting in the seat of mind, observing you, being proud.

proud you have come so far this time, remembering who you really are is a sign.

a sign that you are raising your awareness of self, a level of consciousness above all else.

when you attain this grande state of being, abundance flows effortlessly through your life and can be seen.

"Song"

It flows from our lips and the depths of our soul
it brightens our world takes our heart for a whirl.

when we feel life's pain and emotions run high,
there is little to soothe us like a musical sigh.

sometimes you want quiet and peace to just think,
a heart made of gold enclosed in a bubble of pink.

a song has a way to bring past lives alive,
retrieve memories from places where we once thrived.

just adding some words arranged nice and neat,
to some chords of an instrument, lyric or beat.

It's poems to music that clarify life,
and sometimes they hit home or cut like a knife.

there is nothing so perfect to lift you up like a song,
to take you away or bring you home where you belong.

"Angels"

There are angels in our life right now and not the ghostly kind,
the kind like friends and children or that you meet on a street, like a mime.

the bells ring above me, the chimes of life, I hear them when I write
It's the angels sending messages, so to bring me to the light.

they change our life, they make us think through very unique ways!
I commend them for their creativity and brightening our darkest days.

sometimes an angel comes to us in a disturbed or ill human way,
where we think it's a person we should avoid or run from, set it astray.

teaching us or guiding us isn't always candy and clouds,
our mind is strong and busting through sometimes it takes being loud.

loud is a word used to describe a disturbance in our life,
embrace the loud and you will find you are closer to the guiding light.

If you were an angel and wanted to share a direction someone should go, but couldn't talk or effect freewill but wanted to let them know.

how would you do it, put signs in their life, encourage or nudge them through? Think about this as you move through your day and let angels be your glue.

"He's the One"

I thought it wouldn't work so I almost didn't give it a chance,
but I am stepping out of my comfort zone so I can get a second glance.

he's just a guy, I didn't think he would have so much power over me, when I look into his eyes he draws me in and calls the powers that be.

his lips are perfect, his teeth are too, it's hard to look away, he speaks right to me eye to eye, I could see myself with him every day.

only 2 hours since I met him and a future is formed, he makes me want to change and grow and love like its our last morn.

he is smart, so smart, and intellectually sane, one word out of his mouth and everything about me is tamed.

there has never been a man I would give myself to fully completely and whole, but just in a glimpse of an eye, I can feel the universe pull.

the hard edges I have, the front I put on, it all just becomes an illusion. The thought of being with this man makes me heart jump into confusion.

my independent, forward self who always knows her way, for the first time ever since birth does not have a hand to play.

there is nothing I can say to him now that will express my inner thoughts, he just needs to know that this girl he met has just been thoroughly caught.

I would have his child at 43 without even thinking twice, it sounds so crazy and yet so right, have the stars aligned, please God give advice!?

maybe this is the beginning of me opening up, and it's someone else I am ready for, after all he is 16 behind me but with a 50yr mind and more.

I see myself have total respect for every thought he has and want to walk beside him with all the love I have.

"Shy Soul"

Such a shy soul he said to me, it's like loving more, fearing less and always ready to believe.

I listen to the words that everybody says, the fears, the doubts and worry, the shallow in their breathe.

most of the time they really don't know if what they say is true, they just carry on without a thought, never inspiring new.

I sit inside myself sometimes, watching through my eyes, at the human race communicating like the most words said gets a prize.

I know from lifetimes past and teachers from the other side, that stillness is the only place to grow, everything else allows us to hide.

the biggest growth while being still and quiet watching others, is not to judge but think of love just like you expect of mothers.

if you ever sit and watch the earth you will notice things quite different, how weeds blow in the wind, lady bugs fall, and holes in the leaves at the ends.

you can see the blur from the heat that rises from the cut of tea you drink, or the muscles in your calves so beautiful as you sit cross legged and think.

if you close your eyes you can feel the world and get a glimpse of sun, the sun that shines inside yourself, the inner glowing one.

"Overwhelm"

It's just a feeling, don't know why the sky fill up, we could die. It's overwhelm, an inner thought that clings to our psyche no matter what we were taught.

we take on commitments, say yes instead of no, and want to improve our ability to grow. When we start to complain of time, lacking it, missing it, losing it, yours and mine.

step back from the movie of life and remind, that times is an illusion set down in our mind. This feeling you feel wells up in your chest, makes your mind race fast, anxiety at best.

take 10, close your eyes, breathe deep in and out, to give your inner self a chance to find its way out.

imagine a bubble so big and round stretched out in front of you surrounded by pink. Take all the thoughts that are clogging your mind, see them inside float away and then blink.

you are setting them free all those thoughts of overwhelm, releasing your mind to move on from the helm.

it's not easy to clear a path through your eyes, when your mind is still clouded by dark black skies, the only way through to be self and transparent is by letting each thought float way like the current.

because how things will happen is out of your control, you only can know and believe in your end goal.

let the rest take it's place as the universe works, in your favor no doubt taking refuge in life's twerks.

"Holes in the Leaves"

There is beauty in nothingness, like a hole in a leaf, where the sun shines through like a beautiful motif.

If you sit beneath a tree looking up from the ground,
finding holes in the leaves, you will notice something profound.

there is life in those holes - growing, finding their souls,
insects and spiders and maggots and moles.

building their homes, and making their babies, letting sun rays come through shining down onto daisies.

if a tree is the source for all life of one being, and each leaf is a single incarnation that can be seen. A hole in a leaf is a time in your life where you grow and you stretch, building bridges and fight.

a space that is missing, a lesson to be learned, where character is born and experiences forewarn. So why do some leaves have more holes than another, why do some lives get to flourish and some smothered.

you planned it that way, you are who you are,
from the day you were born, you put thought in your stars.

You are living your ultimate dream,
the one that you had before all could be seen.

So remember this creation is yours and love every moment so it will love you back in fours.

"Openness"

My heart is open, my eyes are too
I don't want to take time to think things through.

go with the feeling that drives you to smile,
it will draw to you love like you've never felt for a while

there is a love that is building, like a root grounds a tree
one that is attached to your soul and is real.

how can this feeling I feel be so real,
when I haven't even laid eyes on this man, so surreal.

although I know it is yet to be found,
I can see being with him will keep me safe and sound.

I have so much to share so much to give,
through the light of the angels I intend to express through how I live.

how I live is a way in which God passes through,
loving and listening and living from truth.

being open even when your heart might be squeezed,
that feeling you have when you've put it on the line and then someone leaves.

the realization afterward it was all worth the trip,
the smiles and laughter and experiences you get.

there is nothing more full and satisfying then to open your heart,
wake up every morning with a grande fresh start.

with the expectation it will be the best day yet,
your life on a platter to be caught by a net.

people wait for cupid to find them and shoot, when it's inside the heart that carries arrows to be sent out like a bag of loot.

everything created outside of ourselves,

things that we wait for, hope for, to come to us with bells.

all of this comes from our imagination and mind,
sent out to the world from ourselves until we find.

we find that we will wait till the ends of the earth,
for the answers we seek but they are in ourselves from birth!

"Chimes"

If you sit beneath a chime and listen to its dance,
the sounds will be like magic bouncing around without a chance.
a change to catch a glimmer of a pattern in the music,
it's different every time you listen mesmerizing as it finds some limericks.

rhythm is a funny thing, to find it in a human being,
they have to be in tune with life, to flow and sway and catch the light.

to play the music in this life,
the kind that set's you above all strife.

it's a wonderful spiritual place to be,
and when you embrace it, it will set you free.

we could all learn a thing from a wind chime hanging low,
blowing in the wind, letting all its pieces swing real slow.

It's the subtle movement really small,
that makes the biggest sound of all.

when the chimes ring true in life,
sometimes we listen sometimes we create strife.

there is always a small breeze before the big wind blows in,
to warn us or hold us to honor our sin!

it's up to us to listen to the signs of the chimes,
embracing each moment we are alive crossing all of the lines.

"Train to Nowhere"

She wants to change herself and the world,
a vibrant woman only 46 years old

her body used to its very core,
her soul abused till it has no more.

to make a difference in this life is her goal,
to be a mom to lift a kids life out of its hole.

what is her souls path, she wonders aloud,
to save someone, to make her mom proud?

there are many paths her life could take,
understanding each one and which could be a mistake.

the journey begins when she finally lets go,
lets go of her anger with herself and her EGO.

her ego is keeping her soul all locked up,
in has-beens, wishes and wants run a-muck!

"My Love"

A tear drops from my eye one day,
as I think about your soul and how it came my way.

we have lived so many lives together,
hurting, loving living – our souls tethered!

when I am quiet and I think of you,
I transcend to a place that is always true.

when life comes in and shows itself in its false illusions and material minds, our connection breaks down, animosity grows, lies and deceit, manipulation begins to confine.

I love the very essence of you, I hate the very earth part of you.

who are you this time that you make me feel this way,
this place in my heart that I will not let you take away.

sometimes I stay away because I know if I get near,
your heart will break me down and I will love you far and near.

you are my soul mate that I cannot be with
you are my friend that I cannot talk with
you are my lover that I cannot love with
you are my mind that I cannot think with
you are the one that I will always love…
and cherish the moments on this earth and up above.

my cold hard words cut deep when we are together,
yet my heart gets into your soul when our bodies touch – it can't be measured.

since the moment we met, our eyes locked, our bodies touched,
something deep was stirred inside me that I knew was more than lust.

it is true that I have thought about our lives from the beginning of time, and how we always find each other because your heart is always part of mine!

"Trees"

From the trees, I get my nourishment, my fearlessness, my valor.
they sway my way when I walk by, just to tell me indirectly "don't be a coward"

I love to watch the trees, they have so much personality and character,
it is them I turn to when things aren't perfect to see their leaves turn color.

each color dancing in the sun can convey more words than humans,
It's easy though they just simply allow and heal through movement.

like a tree we grow from a source so invisible,
into someone and something so amazing it's incredible.

we could learn from a tree, how there is no judgment,
no sadness or scarcity, just enjoying each moment.

it's the trees that define what it is to be free,
to live on our own, love our neighbor's, just me "ME"

"My Man"

He carries himself with the confidence and trust that he knows,
who he is from his head to his toes.

this man I call mine looks at me in a way,
where everyone else in the room fades to gray.

his tall, dark hair that I love to run my hands through,

he smiles at me real big and my guard drops to the floor,
my heart is open and I want so much more.

when he gets near it is magic full of electricity and fire,
when we kiss it sends tingles up and down with desire

he is practical too, such a thinker and happy,
Shares all his thoughts on life and sometimes gets sappy.

I love when he holds me real tight and so close,
it's comforting and loving and sexy and safe feeling the most.

he is reliable, my new man and I love that he's fun,
he can play with eh kids and then go with me on a run.

he's cultured and friendly to all those he meets,
living with no predigests or judgment I can see.

he loves to be with family and spend time with me,
we laugh and we love and we are ok to just "Be"

my man thinks that I am the most beautiful woman he has ever seen,
and tells me this daily, each morning, day and evening.

one day will know that my man has arrived,
he will bring me some flowers and on that same day I will cry.

these flowers I receive will have one red large bloom,
so beautiful and fragrant it will smell up the room.

our love will be so strong no one can break,
it will thrive through the years and I will be in bliss, marriage and cake.

my man will try anything I want in the bed, a lover inside, reading signs,
leading and being led.

sometimes I sit in the lap of my man,
he holds me and strokes at my hair and my hand.

we look at each other, staring into our eyes,
until one of us kisses and the other one sighs.

I would have some more children if that's what he wanted,
I'm open to everything when it comes to his needs and wants.

I will give of my heart to this man – every single inch of it,
until death do us part, open arms, heart, mind, soul and body will be in it!

until this day when I meet my new man,
I will live life to the fullest and enjoy all I can.

"Sending Love"

I sent him love, he does not know it,
he feels some comfort, some joy and he shows it.

a warmth comes over him real subtle,
my angels have spoken, listened to my pink bubble.

I have closed my eyes and got in a place,
of solitude, warmth and grace.

I focused on thinking and sending love,
to surround him and be with him like ten Gods from above.

I imagine him smiling and happy and playing,
the sparkle in his eyes when he knows life is there for him at his feet laying!

he feels this amazing and comforting glow,
just doesn't realize that it came from an angel who knows!

I do this once daily to someone I know,
someone I love and feel joy for, who's low.

they never know how they have come to feel joy,
they only think sometimes God is playing with them like a toy.

I expect nothing in return, no call or text or wanting or yearn
it's an act of kindness that needs no explanation,
just a thought that is directed at a particular incarnation!

so when you feel that a light has been turned on,
a smile grows, a breeze blows or you hear a song.

it's me sending love to your deepest self,
healing your soul with love and wealth.

"No Man is an Island"

As he sits on his own trying to be made of stone,
his eyes tell the truth of how he feels all alone.

The whites of his eyes, the crystal blue inners,
the tear that forms droplets from years of being a sinner.

If only a special someone would come cracking through,
all the walls he has placed on each side, old and new.

years of disappointment, let downs and change,
have put this beautiful man standing in front of me in a cage.

I look at him closely, I listen to his words,
he wows me with his candor, his style, he seems perturbed.

I observe all his movement, this masterpiece on an island,
he needs me to greet him, love him, keep smiling.

what is the pain that has brought him to this space,
I would take it away if I could and put love in its place.

no man is an island he needs someone near,
a woman, a lover, a friend, someone dear.

I am a woman who is drawn to this man,
the man on an island all his own made of sand.

the sand can all crumble with the drop of a hat,
and change your whole life for the better, imagine that.

"Independence"

To be able to do, to create, to perform,
to lead without a leader giving instruction or scorn.

independence has a meaning with a thousand sides,
it allows for achievement and privacy and taking great strides.

it's a value that most wish they could have in abundance,
versus leaning on others to the point of indebtedness.

it is a gift to be able to stand on your own,
to think independent be your own person on your throne.

there is also some loneliness set deep inside,
the desire to detach from others is relentless and you can't hide.

when you get this urge to be on your own,
not go with others, pick up your own stones.

it bothers your soul, sometimes you want to hang with the crowd.
the inner "you" pushes and pulls and gets loud.

until finally for no apparent reason at all,
you disconnect from him/her/everyone and fall.

but fall is a metaphor for withdraw to yourself,
to think and be quiet and gain inner wealth.

sometimes that wealth comes with a price,
elusiveness at its best, lacking relationships in life.

the lesson to be learned while we are here on this earth,
is to accept we are one, all the same from the same source.

on that note we can roam independent of others,
but love close to one another without feeling smothered.

it's the freedom to live without confinement in our heart,
because we feel all the love each person emanates from the start.

"Selfless Hero"

The way a mother looks at you, can make you, break you, or force the truth,

or one day you may even find, a mother that looks all sweet and kind,
but underneath smiles and help, she creates an environment where you think for yourself.
a place of love, a caring home, a helpful heart, where no judgment is felt

I found this mother before I was born,
lifetimes ago when my heart was torn.

I know that I picked her to birth me and say,
"I love you so much each and every day"

because it is not possible to just happen upon,
a mother, a friend, a guide through this life,
that cares for me so deeply she would give her own life.

but I did, I found her, or she found me!
and all of my sisters and brother – but now we are only three.

standing up to your mother is a proud moment in life,
for she has instilled in you what is needed to handle strife.

there are moments I know in my 43 years,
that I asked her advice while shedding tears.

I wanted an answer, a yellow brick road,
when she reminded me in her own way "don't be scared off by something that looks like a toad"

so life has become easy to accept right and wrong,
just stop labeling it and live it and it will play like a song.

I wish for my mother to know on this day,
how much she is loved and what a big part she has played.

Happy Birthday MOM, because the day you arrived,
was the day God looked down at all the earth and said "now I'm alive"

Poems to be continued…in book 2

Note from the Author: Meaning of the Coconut

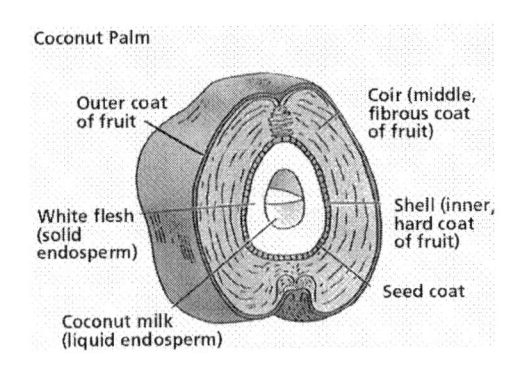

Coconut Palm
- Outer coat of fruit
- Coir (middle, fibrous coat of fruit)
- White flesh (solid endosperm)
- Shell (inner, hard coat of fruit)
- Seed coat
- Coconut milk (liquid endosperm)

~ Consciousness and the Coconut ~

The fruit of the coconut contains a kernel or a seed surrounded by a shell. The seed (i.e. coconut milk) is what most people think about when one says "coconut". There are actually four parts to the coconut fruit – the outer shell surrounding the seed can be removed intact. The seed of the dry coconut shrinks inside the shell and becomes separated from the shell and there is now a distance between the shell and seed. The seed contains the hard shell and a white meat can be eaten and the liquid the coconut milk can be drunk to give life.

A similar thing occurs with our consciousness. Our consciousness creates a vehicle for the physical experience (the body) and then believes it is the vehicle. It believes the shell, the vehicle in the form of the body and the seed, the awareness that created the vehicle are one. However, there will come a time when the consciousness becomes aware, when it becomes ripe. That, it is, the creator separates from its creation. We call it death. In death there is a distance or detachment between the body (shell) and the consciousness (seed) inhabiting the body.

A similar thought occurs with the ego. The ego too is a shell used by the consciousness to define itself and it too can be separated from the consciousness (seed). The essence that is "us" is what creates the identity for the experience it has by the experiences it has. That is, what we experience defines who we think we are. Ideally when we die, the ego created as a result of being in the body also dies. However, many hold on to the ego whole or in part after death of the physical body.

The body is like the shell of the coconut seed and the ego is like the hard outer shell of the seed. The ego can be separated from the essence that gives life. We have a choice, we can wait till we die and have the consciousness and ego separated from the body and wander around the universe as that seed ready to create a new life in the identify we have created. OR, we can if we wish separate our awareness from our ego before body physically dies. This is what it means to transcend the ego using our creative power. Breaking the shell of the seed allows us to create a different life than the one creating the seed and allows us to step out of the past.

CONTEST 2015

Contest name: "Who am I"

Deadline for submissions: April 6, 2015

Contest Rules: Write a poem with the title "Who am I" and let your imagination flow, whatever you feel at the time you write it as the answer to "who you are". No more than 2000 words, only one submission per person.

Where to send:
MAIL TO: 7371 Atlas Walk Way #142, Gainesville VA 20155
EMAIL TO: forbzhouse@gmail.com
ATTN: Contest 2015

Who qualifies for submissions: Anyone, everyone, any age from 1-200

Contest Winner: Most original, vulnerable, open, exposed poem will win. Winner will be chosen on April 6, 2015.

Contest Prize: $1,000

Please be prepared to be published once chosen, this poem will be in my next book and published with your name as Author all rights reserved for FREE

Please be prepared to be interviewed if chosen

FORBZ HOUSE LLC
7371 Atlas Walk Way #142
Gainesville, VA 20155
www.forbzhouse.com
forbzhouse@gmail.com